LESSONS ON CHRISTIAN LIVING

NAVPRESS
A MINISTRY OF THE NAVIGATORS
P.O. BOX 35001, COLORADO SPRINGS, COLORADO 80935

OUR GUARANTEE TO YOU

We believe so strongly in the message of our books that we are making this quality guarantee to you. If for any reason you are disappointed with the content of this book, return the title page to us with your name and address and we will refund to you the list price of the book. To help us serve you better, please briefly describe why you were disappointed. Mail your refund request to: NavPress, P.O. Box 35002, Colorado Springs, CO 80935.

The Navigators is an international Christian organization. Our mission is to reach, disciple, and equip people to know Christ and to make Him known through successive generations. We envision multitudes of diverse people in the United States and every other nation who have a passionate love for Christ, live a lifestyle of sharing Christ's love, and multiply spiritual laborers among those without Christ.

NavPress is the publishing ministry of The Navigators. NavPress publications help believers learn biblical truth and apply what they learn to their lives and ministries. Our mission is to stimulate spiritual formation among our readers.

ISBN 08910-91629

Scripture quotations are from the *Holy Bible: New International Version*® (NIV®). Copyright © 1973, 1978, 1984 by International Bible Society. Used by permission of Zondervan Bible Publishers.

Printed in the United States of America

31 32 33 34 35 / 07 06 05 04 03

FOR A FREE CATALOG OF
NAVPRESS BOOKS & BIBLE STUDIES,
CALL 1-800-366-7788 (USA)
OR 1-416-499-4615 (CANADA)

As you grow in the Christian life it is important to continue studying the Bible regularly and learning how to practice the basics of Christian living. In *Lessons on Christian Living* you will learn about eight principles and promises God has given you as his son or daughter, and the corresponding responsibilities and privileges you have in living a life that pleases God.

You may find it best to take a few of the study questions each day, rather than trying to do the entire lesson in one sitting. This will help you have a regular intake of the word of God. And remember to use spare moments each day for reviewing your verses. Master each memory verse perfectly, word for word.

For effective Bible study it is helpful to have an easy-to-read Bible, a dictionary, and a quiet place to study.

1

PUTTING
CHRIST FIRST

Review the following verses from *Lessons on Assurance*, and check them off after quoting them correctly from memory.

1 John 5:11-12____   1 John 1:9____
John 16:24____   Proverbs 3:5-6____
1 Corinthians 10:13____

MEMORIZE MATTHEW 6:33

Putting Christ First
    "But seek first his kingdom and his righteousness, and all these things will be given to you as well."

Matthew 6:33

God has given us many privileges. But we also have certain responsibilities. The Bible tells us what God expects of us. Our response should be to obey him and to thank him for all he has done for us.

Many promises in the Bible are unconditional. But most of those which concern our growth as Christians are conditional upon our obedience to his will. *Lessons on Christian Living* highlights eight of these responsibilities which will help you build the foundation for a healthy Christian life.

Who will you live your life for? What has first place in your thoughts and plans? Jesus often challenged his disciples to consider their commitment to him and his kingdom. He said, "If anyone would come after me, he must deny himself and take up his cross daily and follow me. For whoever wants to save his life will lose it, but whoever loses his life for me will save it" (Luke 9:23-24).

Following him in this way may mean struggles and trials, but also the privilege of resting in Christ: "Come to me," Jesus

5

said, "all who are weary and burdened, and I will give you rest. Take my yoke upon you and learn from me, for I am gentle and humble in heart, and you will find rest for your souls. For my yoke is easy and my burden is light" (Matthew 11:28-30).

As you memorize and apply Matthew 6:33, seek to know Christ better every day. As you put him, his will, and his work first in your daily life, you will begin to fully experience God's love and care, for he has promised to provide all of your daily needs.

EXPLORING MATTHEW 6:33

What are "these things"? (Look up Matthew 6:25-32.)

_____

_____

Are these necessities or luxuries? Explain your answer.

_____

_____

_____

What has God promised to do if you put his interests first in your life?

_____

_____

"SEEK FIRST HIS KINGDOM AND HIS RIGHTEOUSNESS"

1. What does God want us to do?
   Psalm 37:3

   _____

   Psalm 37:4

   _____

   Psalm 37:5

   _____

2. From 1 Samuel 12:24 give one reason for serving the Lord with all your heart.

   _____

   _____

3. Read 1 Samuel 15:22. What does God desire more than sacrifice?

_____

_____

4. How should we obey God's commands, according to these verses:
Psalm 119:34

_____

Psalm 119:60

_____

5. In 2 Timothy 3:16, what did Paul say is God's means for training us in righteousness?

_____

"ALL THESE THINGS WILL BE GIVEN TO YOU AS WELL"

6. Read Ephesians 3:20-21. How much do you think God can do for you?

_____

_____

7. In Isaiah 40:11, how does God promise to treat his people?

_____

_____

8. Read Philippians 4:4 and 4:6. List two things we are instructed to practice as believers.

_____

_____

9. How does Philippians 4:7 describe the result of applying Philippians 4:4 and 4:6?

_____

_____

10. What was Paul's attitude towards his circumstances in Philippians 4:11-13?

_____

How was he able to do this?

_____

_____

11. According to Matthew 6:8, how well does God know your present needs?

_____

WRITE OUT MATTHEW 6:33 FROM MEMORY.

_____

_____

_____

_____

APPLYING MATTHEW 6:33

Take a moment to pray that God will help you give his kingdom and his righteousness first priority in all areas of your life.

From Matthew 6:25-32 list any needs which you want to trust God for. Claim his promise in Matthew 6:33 for meeting these needs, and pray about them. Place a check here when you have done this: ___ .

2
HIS STRENGTH

Review the following verses, and check them off after quoting
them correctly from memory.

1 John 5:11-12___   1 John 1:9___
John 16:24___   Proverbs 3:5-6___
1 Corinthians 10:13___   Matthew 6:33___

MEMORIZE PHILIPPIANS 4:13

His Strength
    I can do everything through him who gives me
strength.

Philippians 4:13

Occasionally you may experience failure and discouragement.
But the Scriptures remind us of the Christian's true source of
strength. Paul recorded God's promise this way: "My grace is
sufficient for you, for my power is made perfect in weakness"
(2 Corinthians 12:9).

Centuries ago, God told his people, "Do not fear, for I am
with you; do not be dismayed, for I am your God. I will
strengthen you and help you; I will uphold you with my
righteous right hand" (Isaiah 41:10). This promise is just as
sure for us today.

In all the trials and challenges you face, God's presence can
sustain you.

We see this promise of God's strength throughout Scripture, as in Proverbs 18:10—"The name of the Lord is a strong
tower; the righteous run to it and are safe."

As you memorize Philippians 4:13, boldy claim the Lord's
strength for every challenge and opportunity in your daily life,
and watch him work.

EXPLORING PHILIPPIANS 4:13

List some things you face which you cannot do apart from
Christ's strength.

_____

_____

_____

_____

According to this verse, how should you approach these things?

_____

_____

_____

"I CAN DO EVERYTHING"

1. Read 1 Corinthians 1:26-31. Why does God often choose
   "ordinary" people to accomplish great things for him?

   _____

   _____

2. According to John 15:5, what can we accomplish apart from
   Christ?

   _____

   What prerequisite for bearing fruit is mentioned in John
   15:5?

   _____

3. What additional requirement for bearing fruit is listed in
   John 15:7?

   _____

   _____

4. Read 2 Corinthians 12:9. Should we ever allow a weakness or
   an inability to cause lasting discouragement?

   _____

   Why not?

   _____

   _____

5. What did Paul thank God for in 2 Corinthians 2:14?

_____

_____

_____

6. What three gifts from God are listed in 2 Timothy 1:7?

_____

_____

"THROUGH HIM WHO GIVES ME STRENGTH"

7. How did Moses describe the Lord in Exodus 15:2?

_____

_____

8. Read Nehemiah 8:10. According to Nehemiah, what is our source of strength?

_____

9. How did David describe the Lord in Psalm 18:1?

_____

From Psalm 18:2 list the reasons why David thought of God as a source of strength.

_____

_____

_____

10. According to Romans 5:8, what did Christ do for us when we were still sinners?

_____

11. Read Ephesians 3:16-19. How does God strengthen us?

_____

_____

What is the result of this strengthening process?

_____

_____

_____

12. Read 2 Timothy 4:16-18. Why did the Lord strengthen Paul?

_____

_____

What confidence did Paul gain as a result of this experience?

_____

_____

WRITE OUT PHILIPPIANS 4:13 FROM MEMORY.

_____

_____

APPLYING PHILIPPIANS 4:13

List one activity, project, or task in the next week in which you
will need to consciously claim the promise of Philippians 4:13,
and actively rely upon Christ's strength.

_____

_____

_____

_____

3

GOD'S WORD

Review the following verses, and check them off after quoting them correctly from memory.

1 John 5:11-12____	Proverbs 3:5-6____
John 16:24____	Matthew 6:33____
1 Corinthians 10:13____	Philippians 4:13____
1 John 1:9____	

MEMORIZE PSALM 119:9,11

God's Word
   How can a young man keep his way pure? By living according to your word. . . . I have hidden your word in my heart that I might not sin against you.

Psalm 119:9,11

By having the Scriptures in our heart we can experience victory over sin, and can please God in all areas of life.

As the Apostle Paul said farewell to believers from Ephesus, he committed them to God's care and reminded them that God's word "can build you up and give you an inheritance among all those who are sanctified" (Acts 20:32). The Scriptures give us food for spiritual maturity, and prepare us for our eternity with God.

Not having a regular intake of Scripture will stunt our spiritual growth as surely as improper nourishment harms a child. "Like newborn babes," the Apostle Peter wrote, "crave pure spiritual milk, so that by it you may grow up in your salvation" (1 Peter 2:2).

As you memorize Psalm 119:9,11, meditate on the ways God's word can build you up, and look for evidence in your life of how he is doing this.

EXPLORING PSALM 119:9,11

How can you live a pure life?

_____

_____

What will keep you from sin?

_____

_____

"HOW CAN A YOUNG MAN KEEP HIS WAY PURE?"

1. Read 2 Timothy 3:16-17. What will the Scriptures do in your life?

_____

_____

   What will be the end result of what Scripture does in your life?

_____

_____

_____

2. Read Psalm 1:1-3. Whose counsel should you avoid?

_____

_____

   What attitude should you have toward God's word?

_____

_____

   How will your life be influenced by God's word?

_____

_____

"BY LIVING ACCORDING TO YOUR WORD"

3. What does Joshua 1:8 teach us to do to live according to God's word?

_____

_____

4. What did the psalmist ask God in Psalm 119:18?

_____

_____

5. According to verse 93, what had God's precepts done for the writer of Psalm 119?

_____

_____

"I HAVE HIDDEN YOUR WORD IN MY HEART"

6. Read Psalm 19:7-8 and fill in the chart below.

VERSE	WHAT GOD'S WORD IS	WHAT HIS WORD DOES
7		
7		
8		
8		

7. Read Matthew 4:4. Write in your own words what Jesus said about God's word.

_____

_____

_____

8. How can you apply Colossians 3:16?

_____

_____

_____

_____

_____

9. Read Deuteronomy 6:6-7. What did Moses tell the people to do with God's word?

_____

_____

_____

_____

What is a practical way you can talk about Scripture with others?

_____

_____

_____

_____

_____

"THAT I MIGHT NOT SIN AGAINST YOU"

10. What is the word of God able to do in your heart, according to Hebrews 4:12?

_____

_____

_____

11. What results of abiding in God's word are mentioned in John 8:31-32?

_____

_____

12. Read James 1:22-25. Describe the person who forgets what he sees in God's word.

_____

_____

_____

How did James say we should respond to the word of God?

_____

_____

_____

WRITE OUT PSALM 119:9,11 FROM MEMORY.

_____

_____

_____

_____

_____

APPLYING PSALM 119:9,11

Select one of the verses you have already memorized which you need to apply this week. Now write a prayer request based on this need.

_____

_____

_____

_____

Take a moment to pray and ask God to help you carry out your application of Scripture.

4
LOVE

Review the following verses, and check them off after quoting
them correctly from memory.

1 John 5:11-12___   Proverbs 3:5-6___
John 16:24___   Matthew 6:33___
1 Corinthians 10:13___   Philippians 4:13___
1 John 1:9___   Psalm 119:9,11___

MEMORIZE JOHN 13:34-35

Love

"A new commandment I give you: Love one another.
As I have loved you, so you must love one another. All
men will know that you are my disciples if you love one
another."

John 13:34-35

What is love? John said, "This is love: not that we loved God,
but that he loved us and sent his Son as an atoning sacrifice for
our sins" (1 John 4:10).

God is the source of love, and also the perfect example of
what love is. God *is* love.

His love is sacrificial. Christ's death is an eternal reminder
of this.

God's love is also unconditional. You never have to worry
about it diminishing. It is not dependent on our worthiness to
receive it, for no one deserves God's love—and yet he loves
everyone.

"Dear friends," John wrote, "since God so loved us, we
also ought to love one another" (1 John 4:11). As you
memorize John 13:34-35, think of some ways you can show
God's love to others.

EXPLORING JOHN 13:34-35

What is Christ's new commandment?

_____

_____

_____

Whose example of love are we to follow?

_____

What will result when Christians show one another the same
kind of love Jesus extends to us?

_____

_____

"LOVE ONE ANOTHER"

1. What commandments does Christ emphasize in Matthew
   22:37-39?

   _____

   _____

   _____

2. Read 1 John 4:7. What is the source of love?

   _____

3. Who does God love, according to John 3:16?

   _____

4. What is the result of obeying God's word, according to
   1 Peter 1:22?

   _____

   _____

   How does Peter say we are to love one another?

   _____

"AS I HAVE LOVED YOU"

5. Read John 15:12-13. How did Jesus demonstrate his love?

   _____

   _____

6. Read 1 John 2:5. How did John say God's love is shown in our lives?

_____

_____

7. From 1 John 2:6, what indicates that an individual is rightly related to Jesus Christ?

_____

_____

8. In Galatians 5:13, how did Paul teach Christians to exercise freedom?

_____

_____

9. Read 1 John 4:10 and describe God's love.

_____

_____

_____

10. Read John 13:1-17. Before Jesus gave his followers a new command to love one another (John 13:34-35), how did he demonstrate his love to them?

_____

_____

_____

_____

_____

_____

_____

"YOU MUST LOVE ONE ANOTHER"

11. Read 1 John 3:16-18. From verse 17, describe a practical way we are taught to love our brothers.

_____

_____

21

From 1 John 3:18, describe the kind of love we should express to others.

_____

_____

_____

12. Read 1 Corinthians 13. From verses 4-7 list ways you can become more loving, and use this list for prayer.

_____

_____

_____

_____

_____

"ALL MEN WILL KNOW
THAT YOU ARE MY DISCIPLES"

13. Write out John 13:35 in your own words.

_____

_____

_____

_____

WRITE OUT JOHN 13:34-35 FROM MEMORY.

_____

_____

_____

_____

_____

_____

APPLYING JOHN 13:34-35.

Prayerfully review this chapter. Ask God to remind you of a
fellow Christian to whom you need to extend more love. Then
write a plan for demonstrating your love to this person this
week.

_____

_____

_____

_____

_____

5

GIVING

Review the following verses, and check them off after quoting them correctly from memory.

1 John 5:11-12____   Matthew 6:33____
John 16:24____   Philippians 4:13____
1 Corinthians 10:13____   Psalm 119:9,11____
1 John 1:9____   John 13:34-35____
Proverbs 3:5-6____

MEMORIZE 2 CORINTHIANS 9:7

Giving

Each man should give what he has decided in his heart to give, not reluctantly or under compulsion, for God loves a cheerful giver.

2 Corinthians 9:7

God has inexhaustible riches available for his children. We are heirs to all he possesses, for "if we are children, then we are heirs—heirs of God and co-heirs with Christ" (Romans 8:17).

God is eager to share these riches with us: "He who did not spare his own Son, but gave him up for us all—how will he not also, along with him, graciously give us all things?" (Romans 8:32).

Everything you have is from God. You can show your gratitude to God by generously giving yourself—your time, your possessions, your talents, and your money—to those who have needs.

Giving is sharing what God has given to us. We cannot give more than God will give back to us. Jesus said, "Give, and it will be given to you. A good measure, pressed down, shaken together and running over, will be poured into your lap. For with the measure you use, it will be measured to you'' (Luke 6:38).

As you memorize 2 Corinthians 9:7, think of specific and practical ways to share with others what God has freely given you.

EXPLORING 2 CORINTHIANS 9:7

What attitudes toward giving are pleasing to God?

_____

_____

_____

What attitudes should you avoid?

_____

_____

_____

"EACH MAN SHOULD GIVE WHAT HE HAS DECIDED"

1. Paraphrase 2 Corinthians 9:6

_____

_____

_____

_____

_____

2. What did Jesus say about spiritual treasure and material wealth in Matthew 6:19-21?

_____

_____

_____

_____

_____

3. What warning did Jesus give in Luke 12:15?

_____

_____

Why do you think he issued this warning?

_____

_____

_____

4. According to Acts 20:35, what did Jesus say about giving?

_____

_____

"NOT RELUCTANTLY OR UNDER COMPULSION"

5. Read Matthew 6:1-4 and describe the manner of giving that God blesses.

_____

_____

_____

6. Read Exodus 35:4-5. What attitude does God desire us to have as we give?

_____

_____

7. In 1 Chronicles 29:9, what was the people's response after they gave to God?

_____

How had they given?

_____

8. Read 2 Corinthians 8:9. How should Jesus' example motivate us to give liberally?

_____

_____

_____

9. In 1 Corinthians 16:1-2, what plan did Paul propose for regular giving?

_____

_____

_____

"GOD LOVES A CHEERFUL GIVER"

10. Read Luke 21:1-4. How did Jesus view the widow's small gift?

_____

_____

11. Read 2 Corinthians 9:8-15. What is promised to those who give cheerfully (verse 8)?

_____

_____

What will God do for generous givers (verses 10-11)?

_____

_____

12. From Philippians 4:18-19, list some results of giving to others.

_____

_____

_____

WRITE OUT 2 CORINTHIANS 9:7 FROM MEMORY.

_____

_____

_____

_____

APPLYING 2 CORINTHIANS 9:7.

What has God given you that you can share with others?

_____

_____

Consider your giving in the past. What is a specific way you could increase your giving to God's work or to those in need?

_____

_____

_____

6
THE CHURCH

Review the following verses, and check them off after quoting them correctly from memory.

1 John 5:11-12___   Matthew 6:33___
John 16:24___   Philippians 4:13___
1 Corinthians 10:13___   Psalm 119:9,11___
1 John 1:9___   John 13:34-35___
Proverbs 3:5-6___   2 Corinthians 9:7___

MEMORIZE PSALM 122:1

The Church
     I rejoiced with those who said to me, "Let us go to the house of the Lord."

Psalm 122:1

The church is made up of all true Christians everywhere—and it includes many thousands of local churches. God instituted these local churches to help Christians grow spiritually. You will have fellowship with other believers there—including opportunities to serve and encourage them. You will receive "training in righteousness" (2 Timothy 3:16) as God's word is preached and taught in the local church.
     Scripture teaches us to seek out this kind of fellowship: "Let us not give up meeting together, as some are in the habit of doing, but let us encourage one another—and all the more as you see the Day approaching" (Hebrews 10:24-25).

EXPLORING PSALM 122:1

What is a good attitude to have in a worship service?

___

What do you think made David glad as he considered going to the house of the Lord?

_____

_____

"I REJOICED"

1. Read Acts 2:42-47. How did the early Christians respond to the nurture and fellowship they enjoyed?

_____

_____

2. Why could Paul say in 1 Thessalonians 1:2-3 that he was joyful about the growth of the local church at Thessalonica?

_____

_____

3. In 1 Thessalonians 2:19-20, Paul again said the Thessalonian Christians made him joyful. Read 1 Thessalonians 2:13 and explain the reason for Paul's joy.

_____

_____

_____

"LET US GO TO THE HOUSE OF THE LORD"

4. What did Jesus promise in Matthew 18:19-20 to those who gather in his name?

_____

_____

5. Paul explained one of the church's main purposes in Ephesians 4:11-12. Write out these verses in your own words.

_____

_____

_____

_____

_____

_____

30

6. Read Ephesians 4:13-15. What will be the result in our lives when the church's ministry follows the pattern described in Ephesians 4:11-12?

_____

_____

_____

_____

_____

7. According to Ephesians 4:11-15, who in addition to the pastor is responsible for the growth of Christians in a local congregation?

_____

According to Ephesians 4:15-16, how is the body of Christ built up?

_____

_____

_____

8. In 1 Thessalonians 5:12-13, how did Paul say we should regard our Christian leaders?

_____

_____

How should we follow the example of our spiritual leaders, according to Hebrews 13:7?

_____

_____

9. Read Colossians 1:13-20. Who is the head of the church?

_____

How did Paul describe the church in Colossians 1:18?

_____

10. What is the result of hearing God's word proclaimed, according to Romans 10:17?

_____

_____

11. Read Romans 12:3-16. Summarize what this passage teaches about relationships within the body of Christ.

_____

_____

_____

_____

_____

12. What did Paul long for among the Christians at Rome, according to Romans 15:5-6?

_____

_____

_____

_____

13. What did Jesus especially pray for all believers in John 17:20-23?

_____

_____

_____

WRITE OUT PSALM 122:1 FROM MEMORY.

_____

_____

_____

APPLYING PSALM 122:1

Prayerfully review your study, especially the Scripture passages and ideas which were most helpful to you personally. Write a short paragraph on why the church is important to your spiritual growth.

_____

_____

_____

_____

_____

How can you better serve your local church?

_____

_____

_____

_____

_____

_____

7

GOOD WORKS

Review the following verses, and check them off after quoting them correctly from memory.

1 John 5:11-12____   Philippians 4:13____
John 16:24____   Psalm 119:9,11____
1 Corinthians 10:13____   John 13:34-35____
1 John 1:9____   2 Corinthians 9:7____
Proverbs 3:5-6____   Psalm 122:1____
Matthew 6:33____

MEMORIZE EPHESIANS 2:10

Good Works
> For we are God's workmanship, created in Christ Jesus to do good works, which God prepared in advance for us to do.
>
> Ephesians 2:10

Your salvation wasn't earned by your good deeds. We are all saved by faith, and not by good works (Ephesians 2:8-9). Nevertheless, God wants your life now to be filled with good works—doing what is right and helpful to others. In this we are to follow the example of Jesus, who "went around doing good" (Acts 10:38).

It is faith alone that saves, but the faith that saves is never alone.

Paul wrote that believers should be "careful to devote themselves to doing what is good. These things are excellent and profitable for everyone" (Titus 3:8). As you seek to do God's will through good works, you—and others through you—will profit. And God will be glorified, because he has good works planned especially for you to accomplish.

EXPLORING EPHESIANS 2:10

What do you think "God's workmanship" means?

_____

_____

What are we created for?

_____

_____

What are good works?

_____

_____

_____

_____

"FOR WE ARE GOD'S WORKMANSHIP"

1. Read Titus 3:8. Who should do good works?

   _____

   _____

   Who should benefit from good works?

   _____

   _____

2. According to Ephesians 2:8-9, why don't good works have a part in our salvation?

   _____

   _____

3. Paraphrase Titus 3:14.

   _____

   _____

   _____

   _____

   _____

   _____

4. What should be the result of our good works, according to Matthew 5:14-16?

_____

_____

5. Read Colossians 3:17. As we do good works, who do we represent?

_____

"TO DO GOOD WORKS"

6. What were the following Christians commended for?

Dorcas (Acts 9:36)

_____

_____

Phoebe (Romans 16:1-2)

_____

_____

Epaphras (Colossians 4:12)

_____

_____

7. Read Matthew 25:31-46. List several practical ways in which you can serve Christ by doing good to others.

_____

_____

_____

_____

_____

_____

8. In 1 Peter 2:12, what did Peter say would make nonChristians glorify God?

_____

_____

_____

9. To whom should we do good, according to Galatians 6:10?

_____

_____

10. What ways for doing good are mentioned in the following passages?

Romans 12:13

_____

_____

2 Corinthians 9:7-8

_____

_____

James 1:27

_____

_____

11. In James 2:15-16, what did James say proves our true concern for those in need?

_____

_____

_____

_____

12. Read 2 Timothy 3:16-17. What equips a Christian for every good work?

_____

_____

WRITE OUT EPHESIANS 2:10 FROM MEMORY.

_____

_____

_____

_____

_____

_____

APPLYING EPHESIANS 2:10.

Prayerfully review your study and list several practical good works you could do for someone.

_____

_____

_____

_____

Now write the name of one person for whom you would like to do a good work this week, and circle in your list above the thing you would like to do for this person.

_____

8
WITNESSING

Review the following verses, and check them off after quoting them correctly from memory.

1 John 5:11-12____   Philippians 4:13____
John 16:24____   Psalm 119:9,11____
1 Corinthians 10:13____   John 13:34-35____
1 John 1:9____   2 Corinthians 9:7____
Proverbs 3:5-6____   Psalm 122:1____
Matthew 6:33____   Ephesians 2:10____

MEMORIZE MARK 5:19

Witnessing
  "Go home to your family and tell them how much the Lord has done for you, and how he has had mercy on you."

Mark 5:19

What could you tell someone about how your life has changed because of Christ? Have you thought about how to give a clear explanation of your faith?

Peter wrote, "Always be prepared to give an answer to everyone who asks you to give the reason for the hope that you have" (1 Peter 3:15).

As someone who has experienced God's saving love, you have much to share.

In Mark 5 we read how Jesus encountered a man who was demon-possessed and living in tombs. With power Jesus healed the man.

As Jesus was leaving, the man begged him to let him come along. Jesus' reply—the memory verse for this lesson— was that the man should instead return home and share his new-

41

found life with others. The man did so, and we read in Mark 5:20 that "all the people were amazed."

We too were living in the "tombs" of deadly sin before we accepted Christ as our Savior. And so we also have good news to tell others!

EXPLORING MARK 5:19

What did Jesus tell this man to share with members of his family?

_____

_____

Read Mark 5:2-5 and 5:15. What impact do you think this man's changed life would have on his family?

_____

_____

"TELL THEM HOW MUCH
THE LORD HAS DONE FOR YOU"

1. Read 2 Corinthians 5:20. What does God say we are?

_____

2. In Acts 4:18-20, Peter and John were ordered not to speak or teach in the name of Jesus. Why did Peter and John say they could not obey this order (verse 20)?

_____

_____

3. Write a paragraph summarizing the most important things you believe the Lord has done for you.

_____

_____

_____

_____

_____

_____

_____

_____

4. Read Romans 1:16. Why can we have confidence in speaking to others about the good news of Jesus Christ?

_____

_____

"TELL THEM . . . HOW HE HAS HAD MERCY ON YOU"

5. What important facts do you see in these verses about why and how God saved you?

   Romans 3:23

   _____

   _____

   Romans 6:23

   _____

   _____

   Romans 5:8

   _____

   _____

   John 1:12

   _____

   _____

6. Describe in your own words the truth of Romans 5:1 as you have experienced it in your life.

   _____

   _____

   _____

7. How did Paul summarize the gospel in 1 Corinthians 15:3-4?

   _____

   _____

   _____

8. You are sure to receive a variety of responses as you share your faith with others. Many will raise objections to the gospel, and will not recognize their need of Christ. Read the Scriptures listed on the next page and tell how they apply to the following objections to the gospel:

"I'm basically a good person." (Ephesians 2:8-9, Titus 3:5)

_____

_____

"People from all religions will make it to heaven." (John 14:6, Acts 4:12)

_____

_____

"What about all the Christians I know who are hypocrites?" (Romans 14:12)

_____

_____

"I'll become a Christian someday." (2 Corinthians 6:2, James 4:14).

_____

_____

9. What did Paul request prayer for regarding his witnessing to others (Colossians 4:3-4)?

_____

_____

_____

WRITE OUT MARK 5:19 FROM MEMORY.

_____

_____

_____

_____

_____

APPLYING MARK 5:19

Write here the names of some people you would like to witness to about what Christ has done for you.

_____

_____

_____

Begin to pray regularly for these people, and plan a time you could share the gospel with at least one of them. Briefly describe your plan here.

_____

_____

_____

_____

_____

_____

CONTINUING
IN GOD'S
WORD

To keep growing in Christ you will need a regular intake of God's Word. The following Bible study and Scripture memory tools from NavPress can help you maintain consistency in learning more of God's truth.

BIBLE STUDY

Studies in Christian Living—This is a six-booklet series concentrating on practical principles of discipleship. It is particularly helpful for those with little previous background in the Scriptures.

Design for Discipleship—This seven-book series also focuses on practical discipleship principles, but at a somewhat faster pace and with more probing questions than *Studies in Christian Living*.

God's Design for the Family—Written for married or engaged couples, these Bible studies emphasize a practical understanding of scriptural principles relating to family life. The two books in the series are *Husbands and Wives* and *Parents and Children*.

Thinking Through Discipleship—Christ wants to change not only what we say and do, but the way we think. The character qualities, values, and motives that lie behind our behavior. In this four-booklet series you'll take a closer look at the implications of knowing God, relating differently to others, and becoming more like Jesus on the inside.

SCRIPTURE MEMORY

Topical Memory System—This course helps you establish a lifelong Scripture memory program as you memorize sixty key passages. The *Topical Memory System* is available in four translations of the Bible.

Topical Memory System: Life Issues—Another opportunity to memorize and meditate on Scripture, in twelve areas that touch your everyday life: anger, guilt, depression, perfectionism, stress, and others. Includes articles, questions, and additional Scripture references on all these topics.

GROW IN YOUR WALK WITH GOD.

Lessons on Assurance

This book presents five short Bible studies on basic promises God gives to Christians: assurance of salvation, answered prayer, victory over sin, forgiveness, and guidance. Part of the GROWING IN CHRIST FOLLOW-UP series.

Lessons on Assurance $3

Growing in Christ

Growing in Christ is a combination of *Lessons on Assurance* and *Lessons on Christian Living* and includes verse cards to start a Scripture memory program.

Growing in Christ $6

Get your copies today at your local bookstore, through our website, or by calling (800) 366-7788. (Ask for offer **#2349** or a FREE catalog of NavPress products.)